Literary Newsmakers for Students, Volume 2

Project Editor
Anne Marie Hacht **Editorial**
Ira Mark Milne

Rights Acquisition and Management
Margaret Chamberlain-Gaston and Robyn Young
Manufacturing
Rita Wimberly

Imaging
Lezlie Light, Mike Logusz, and Kelly Quin
Product Design
Pamela A. E. Galbreath **Vendor Administration**
Civie Green **Product Manager**
Meggin Condino © 2006 Gale, a part of Cengage Learning Inc.

Cengage and Burst Logo are trademarks and Gale is a registered trademark used herein under license.

For more information, contact
Gale, an imprint of Cengage Learning

27500 Drake Rd.

Farmington Hills, MI 48331-3535

Or you can visit our Internet site at http://www.gale.com **ALL RIGHTS RESERVED** No part of this work covered by the copyright hereon may be reproduced or used in any form or by any means—graphic, electronic, or mechanical, including photocopying, recording, taping, Web distribution, or information storage retrieval systems—without the written permission of the publisher.

For permission to use material from this product, submit your request via Web at http://www.gale-edit.com/permissions, or you may download our Permissions Request form and submit your request by fax or mail to: *Permissions Department*
Gale, an imprint of Cengage Learning
27500 Drake Rd.
Farmington Hills, MI 48331-3535
Permissions Hotline:
248-699-8006 or 800-877-4253, ext. 8006
Fax: 248-699-8074 or 800-762-4058

Since this page cannot legibly accommodate all copyright notices, the acknowledgments constitute an extension of the copyright notice.

While every effort has been made to ensure the reliability of the information presented in this publication, Gale, an imprint of Cengage Learning does not guarantee the accuracy of the data contained herein. Gale, an imprint of Cengage Learning accepts no payment for listing; and inclusion in the publication of any organization, agency, institution, publication, service, or individual does not imply endorsement of the editors or publisher. Errors brought to the attention of the publisher and verified to the satisfaction of the publisher will be corrected in future editions.

ISBN 13: 978-1-4144-0282-6
ISBN 10: 1-4144-0282-1
ISSN: 1559-9639

This title is also available as an e-book
ISBN-13: 978-1-4144-2930-4, ISBN-10: 1-4144-2930-4
Contact your Gale, an imprint of Cengage Learning representative for ordering information.

Printed in the United States of America

10 9 8 7 6 5 4 3 2 1

Delights & Shadows

Ted Kooser
2004

Introduction

Delights & Shadows (2004) is a highly regarded collection of poetry by one of the best known, most accessible, and most respected poets in the United States. Ted Kooser's Pulitzer Prizewinning bookcontains poems published previously in literary magazines from 1994 to 2004. *Delights & Shadows* sold more than fifty thousand copies, an extraordinary number for a collection of poetry in the United States. Kooser was named Poet Laureate of the United States soon after its publication.

Like much of Kooser's work, the poems in *Delights & Shadows* are written in a simple style with clear language and lucid yet challenging constructions. Kooser has lived much of his life in Iowa and Nebraska, and the poems reflect life as he knows it on the Great Plains. The poems in the collection touch on topics both bleak and celebratory, including impressions of strangers, family, memories, mortality, and history.

Throughout *Delights & Shadows*, Kooser repeatedly notes the unexpected in the smallest of objects, touches, and connections. He contrasts surprising images in his poems to create an emotional response in readers. In the *Library Journal*, reviewer Louis McKee noted, "That he often sees things we do not would be delight enough, but more amazing is exactly what he sees. Nothing escapes him; everything is illuminated." While some critics regard *Delights & Shadows* as the product of a regional writer, others believe that Kooser has transcended his background and reached a universal audience with this collection of poems.

Author Biography

Born on April 25, 1939, in Ames, Iowa, Ted Kooser is the son of Theodore, Sr., and Vera (nee Moser) Kooser. Raised in Iowa, Kooser began writing poetry at an early age and became serious about his poetry as a teenager. Kooser attended Iowa State University in Ames, earning his bachelor's degree in 1962 from Iowa State University. He then spent a year working as a high school teacher in Madrid, Iowa.

In the mid-1960s, Kooser moved to Nebraska to attend graduate school at the University of Nebraska, where he earned a master's degree in English in 1968. He wanted to be a poet but realized he could not support himself and his family by writing poetry. He began working in the insurance industry while a graduate student. Kooser was hired by Bankers Life Nebraska as a correspondent in 1964 and became an underwriter the following year. He held various positions in the insurance industry for the next thirty-five years, reaching the executive ranks. Kooser chose the insurance industry because the demands of work did not sap all of his creativity. He also worked as an adjunct professor of writing at the University of Nebraska from 1970 to 1995.

Kooser rose in the early morning to write for several hours before going to work each day. He was influenced by William Carlos Williams and he believed, like Williams, that poetry should be readily accessible to readers. From his earliest poems, Kooser often expressed a sense that life is fragile. Kooser began publishing poetry in periodicals in the mid-1960s and put out his first collection, *Official Entry Blank*, in 1969. He continued to publish in literary magazines and other periodicals throughout the 1970s, 1980s, and 1990s, while putting together several collections. Kooser won many awards for his writing, such as the Pushcart Prize, the Stanley Kunitz Prize, the James Boatwright Prize, and two fellowships in poetry from the National Endowment for the Arts.

Kooser retired from the insurance business in 1999. In the late 1990s, he developed cancer and stopped writing for a time. Fighting for his health, he began writing again when he started taking walks in the early morning and writing poems based on what he saw. He sent the poems on postcards to his friend Jim Harrison, and they became the book *Winter Morning Walks: One Hundred Postcards to Jim Harrison* (2001). He also returned to the University of Nebraska as a visiting professor of English in 2000.

In 2004, Kooser published his tenth collection of poetry, *Delights & Shadows*, which was awarded the 2005 Pulitzer Prize for Poetry. Beginning in 2004, Kooser was named the thirteenth Poet Laureate of the United States. As poet laureate, he seeks to increase appreciation for poetry in the United States, a task he approaches with gusto in his column "American Life in Poetry." Kooser has continued to publish his own poetry collections, as well as two nonfiction books on writing for aspiring authors, *The Poetry Home Repair Manual: Practical Advice for Beginning Poets* (2005) and *Writing Brave and Free: Encouraging Words for People Who Want to Start Writing* (2006). As of 2006, he lives on a farm near Garland, Nebraska, with his wife Kathleen Rutledge. He continues to write poetry and teach at the University of Nebraska-Lincoln.

Plot Summary

I. *Walking on Tiptoe*

In the first of the four sections in *Delights & Shadows*, the poems are primarily impressionistic sketches of people. The first poem in this section, "Walking on Tiptoe," laments how the many burdens humans carry have forced them to walk more heavily than certain animals that are graceful and ready to spring into motion. At the end of the poem, Kooser notes that humans still sometimes creep silently in the night, like animals, when they walk on tiptoe through the house.

Kooser continues to observe the human experience in the next poem, "Tattoo." In this poem, he describes an older man shopping at a yard sale. The man has a tattoo of "a dripping dagger held in the fist of a shuddering heart" on his shoulder. The poet senses that neither the man nor the tattoo is as bold or vital as it was once.

In "At the Cancer Clinic," Kooser observes a woman who cannot walk to an exam room without the assistance of two others and a nurse, who urge the patient on. The woman is dignified, the nurse is calm, and the people in the waiting room are respectful. Kooser portrays the situation as one exemplifying grace and kindness.

The next poem, "Student," describes a young

male student who seems like a turtle moving forward with awkward determination into his future. Kooser compares the student's backpack to a shell and his chin to a beak as he enters the library with the same effort that a turtle shows in leaving the sea.

"Gyroscope" also begins with a first-person observation. Kooser observes a young girl playing with a gyroscope on an enclosed porch. This small event takes place on a sunny day in February, with spring inching closer. Kooser draws a comparison between the girl with her plaything and the balance of the changing seasons.

Kooser returns to the evidence of age in "New Cap." Each short line of the poem focuses on the corduroy cap that an eighty-six-year-old man bought when he was young, and which he still wears. Kooser conveys that what is literally and figuratively contained in the cap—the man's head and its contents—has changed, becoming smaller and more fragile.

In the next poem, "Cosmetics Department," Kooser describes two beautiful women together in what seems like an eternal pose. This poem contrasts with "New Cap" in color and content. The first word in "New Cap" is "Brown," describing the color of the old man's cap. The five two-line stanzas that make up "Cosmetics Department" also make use of color imagery. The women Kooser describes wear black and look like they should be decoration on a white cup. White is used as an image of their youth: "The white moth of timelessness flutters about them."

The five lines of "Biker" create a poem of motion. Kooser describes a motorcycle rider returning to motion after being stopped at a traffic light. Again invoking animal imagery, Kooser contrasts the biker's movements with "the old dog of inertia" who "gets up with a growl and shrinks out of the way."

"The Old People" is more abstract and seems to view the aged in a different light than the other poems in this section. After describing them physically in the first line ("Pantcuffs rolled, and in old shoes"), Kooser uses metaphors to compare aging to going into the night, away from the light of youth.

The next two poems are similar to each other in their use of weather images and movement. The ten lines of "In January" contrast the only light in town, coming from a small Vietnamese cafe, with the winter wind blowing through and shaking windows. "A Rainy Morning" focuses on "a young woman in a wheelchair" pushing herself through the rain. Kooser compares the motion of her hands with the movements and rhythmic chords of a pianist's.

The short poem "Mourners" gives Kooser's impressions of people after a funeral. After describing the shady churchyard setting and the physical characteristics of the mourners, "White shirt cuffs and collars," the poet focuses on an irony of funerals: The people gathered are saying farewell to one life yet greeting the others present, still alive and holding on to their connections with one another.

The section ends with "Skater," in which the poet describes a young woman figure skating. While the poem focuses on her physical movements on the ice, the sounds her skates make, and the clothes she wears, Kooser ends by relating her skating to a flash of maturity: "skating backward right out of that moment, smiling back / at the woman she'd been just an instant before."

II. The China Painters

Many of the poems in this section focus on life in the Midwest and Kooser's own family in Iowa. The first poem is also the title poem, "The China Painters." This poem describes the well-worn tools of china painters, including the brushes and colors used to create delicate flowers. Kooser then notes that this art has gone out of fashion but returns "like a garden" when the good dishes are used for Sunday dinner.

"Memory" is a swirl of images that uses a tornado as a metaphor for memories. Kooser describes a tornado cutting through a farm, disrupting its fields, machines, barns, animals, and a family eating dinner. He describes the tornado removing the roof of the house, picking up the people one by one, and gazing at them before returning them to their place. The poem's last words reveal that the tornado is the poet: "its crowded, roaring, dusty funnel, / and there at its tip was the nib of a pen."

Kooser examines a place resonant with the past

in the three stanzas of "Ice Cave." In the first stanza, he describes a cool cave where ice harvested from local waterways during the winter was stored. In the second stanza, Kooser tells readers that in summer some of the winter ice still remained and the cave was used by families as a cool escape. He concludes by describing the visitors' walk home with the cold from the cave seeming to follow them.

Several of the poems in the heart of this section focus on Kooser's own family. "Mother" is written in the first person, with Kooser describing the details of nature and life on an April day a month after his mother's death. In the five stanzas, Kooser mourns what he has lost but thanks her for his life and for giving him a perspective that allows him to move on.

"A Jar of Buttons" is another domestic poem, written in two-line stanzas. Describing a long-used jar of buttons, "a core sample / from the floor of the Sea of Mending," Kooser continues the nautical metaphor in his description of the women who use these buttons to maintain their families' clothes. He writes that they work on "decks sometimes salted by tears," like sailors on the ship of life.

Kooser returns to a more personal past with "Dishwater" and "Zenith." In "Dishwater," he describes in detail his grandmother's routine chore of throwing out the dirty dishwater, emphasizing the physical actions involved. "Zenith" recalls another memory in which Kooser and his sister would sit with their grandmother in her parlor and listen to news of the war on the radio.

In this section, Kooser also writes several poems about responsible adult men. "The Necktie" describes a man as he dresses for work. Though clearly a serious man embarking on serious business, there is a moment of private playfulness as he waves "hello / to himself with both hands" as he ties his tie. "Father," written on May 19, 1999, is an ode to his father on what would have been his ninety-seventh birthday. The poet is glad that his father is not alive and unhappy, but still misses him and reminisces about a story his father used to tell.

Some of the poems about Kooser's past focus more ambiguous people. While the woman at the center of "Depression Glass" is not identified, Kooser makes clear that she is someone from the past with whom he had a close relationship. He describes times in which they drank coffee in carefully collected cups, now reserved for company, and shared the week's news and gossip. Kooser seems to have a similar relationship with the woman at the heart of "Applesauce." He begins by describing what he liked about the process of making homemade applesauce before offering details about the meticulous earnestness of the woman who makes it.

"Creamed Corn" follows "Applesauce," and is linked to it by a mention of Iowa. Employing a more prose-like style, Kooser talks about racism in Iowa. Though white locals were comfortable with the black families that had lived there for a long time, they were more suspicious of the Jamaicans who came to work at a local canning plant in the

1940s. Kooser bemoans gossip that the Jamaicans tampered with the creamed corn, ending his poem proclaiming, "Years later ... our ignorance spoils the creamed corn."

In the next poem, Kooser talks specifically about his family again. "Flow Blue China" is an ode to his aunt who gave him the china she used for much of her life. Kooser compares the ever-serving flowers on the china to his aunt, honoring her existence after she "has slipped beyond the thin line at the edge." In "Pearl," he tells the story of a visit with his mother's cousin. In one of the longest poems in *Delights & Shadows*, Kooser travels to Pearl's house in Iowa to tell her that his mother has died. She tells him stories about his mother and about her own poor health. In the course of their conversation, Pearl tells him about the people she sees in her house cataloguing her possessions who she knows are not real, and he suggests that she go to her doctor. After the visit has ended and the poet has left, Kooser leaves the reader with Pearl's imaginary people: "the others stepped out of the stripes of light / and resumed their inventory."

The idea of the nearness of death is also present in "Old Cemetery." Kooser observes the poor groundskeeping job someone has done at a cemetery. Detailing the results of the rushed, careless job, the poet considers the perspectives of the deceased, imagining their relief as the groundskeeper's truck leaves and the weeds rise again. The section ends with "A Winter Morning," a quiet four-line poem set in a farmhouse and focusing on the sound of a kettle and the sight of a tiny flame.

III. Bank Fishing for Bluegills

The poems in this section are primarily about history, and they imagine looking at the past with the neutrality of objects. The section opens with its title poem, which begins with the image of an "empty aluminum boat" in the water. Kooser uses this image as a metaphor for a dying man; both are tethered lightly to the world. The rest of the poem links the boat to the man, his pastime, his appearance, and his fading, tenuous hold on life.

The next poem, "Four Civil War Paintings by Winslow Homer," opens with Homer's quote from newspaper in 1865 about how a painter's work can be seen like nature if the painter is more of an observer than a reflector. The poem is divided into four parts, each examining a different painting and offering a brief explanation of its subject. Through the poem as a whole, Kooser looks at four perspectives of the Civil War.

"1. SHARPSHOOTER" portrays a Union soldier sitting in the tree at the ready. Kooser begins by calling it a "painting of waiting," then describes what he sees in the painting itself: the man ready to shoot. Next, "2. THE BRIGHT SIDE" features five black Union teamsters who haul the necessities of war. Kooser contrasts their appearance of dark weariness with the light, bright objects in the background. In "3. PRISONERS FROM THE

FRONT," the poet describes three Confederate soldiers as they wait for a Union general to determine their fates. Kooser believes that one young soldier would spoil this picture for the general if the painter had let him. "4. THE VETERAN IN A NEW FIELD," the shortest of the four parts, focuses on a single man, a veteran of the war, working in a wheat field during the summer.

Beginning with "Turkey Vultures," an impression of the animals flying lazily around in the air above, taking a break from their business of attending to death, Kooser moves through a number of descriptive poems about objects and animals. "Pegboard" compares the outlines for the tools on a board with French cave drawings from prehistory, while "At the County Museum" uses ten two-line stanzas to describe an old hearse, ruminate on its past, and remember death. "Casting Reels" and "Praying Hands" also ponder the title objects, commonly found for re-sale. Kooser wonders about the uses for both.

"Horse" is a six-line poem about the appearance of a horse, highlighting its majesty. "*Lobocraspis griseifusa*" is a "tiny moth who lives on tears" harvested at night from a sorrow-filled dream, unburdening the dreamer. Kooser then returns to objects, beginning with "Home Medical Dictionary," which focuses on not on the dictionary itself but on how it is used by the elderly as they fearfully seek to understand their pain.

In "In the Hall of Bones," Kooser describes the skeletons of three different animals and one human that are put together on display. The poet emphasizes the differences between the human and animal skeletons by ending with the observation that the human skeleton "is the only one / in which once throbbed a heart / made sad by brooding on its shadow." Kooser sees a sheep's pain in "A Jacquard Shawl," carefully woven in 1778 with wool taken from sheep that were killed by dogs. The poet includes the perspective of the weaver, imagining that her loom echoes the sounds of the attack.

The next two poems, which face each other in the text, contrast darkness and light. In "Telescope," Kooser compares a telescope to a pipe in a dam "that takes off some of the pressure," to keep "the straining wall of darkness" from crashing down. "A Box of Pastels" uses first-person perspective to describe the title object, once owned by the artist Mary Cassatt. Cassatt primarily painted domestic scenes, and Kooser notes that the pale colors are worn down while the darker shades are barely used. Kooser leaves the experience feeling lighter himself.

The poet returns to nature with "Old Lilacs" and "Grasshoppers." He anticipates the change from spring to summer as it relates to horses in "Old Lilacs." After observing how skinny horses are as they look for food in the changing weather of spring, Kooser spends the last stanza painting the month of May as a time of greenery which will make the horses fit and attractive again. "Grasshoppers" is a poem about farmers' struggles. Kooser compares the size and color of the crop-eating pests to an object from the drought of the 1930s, a pencil his grandfather used for keeping track of rainfall. The poet compares the way grasshoppers sound when they are in the grass to the sound of raindrops, noting the irony.

The last poem in the section, "The Beaded Purse," is a narrative poem set in a time when train and wagon travel were the norm. Kooser tells the story of a man in rural Kansas who meets a train carrying his daughter's remains. She left the family to become an actress in the East and told them she was successful and happy. He sees that she has aged severely and that her purse contains no money. He puts a few dollars inside and takes his daughter's body home.

IV. That Was I

Many of the poems in this section focus on themes of perception and hope as well as loss and love. The section opens with the title poem, "That Was I." In each of the three stanzas, Kooser describes a scene in which an older man, himself, explores lonely sites. He knows that observers might see him and think of decay and age, but his thoughts are of hope and control. Each stanza ends in the refrain, "Yes, that was I."

Between the brief "Screech Owl," which equates the loud sound this small owl makes with hopefulness, and the simple "The Early Bird," which describes the joy humans get from the sound of a bird singing in the rain, sits "A Spiral

Notebook." In this poem, Kooser equates aging with not needing a five-subject notebook because of the lack of subjects in one's life. The only subject he focuses on is the notebook itself and what it could mean. "On the Road" is another meditation on the importance, or unimportance, of holding things or letting them go. The poet describes finding a pretty rock while walking, and he writes that his inner voice tells him to drop it and continue on his path.

Kooser turns to observation once again in "A Washing of Hands." In this poem, he watches a woman washing her hands, focusing his metaphorical language on the water and how her hands manipulate it. He describes the water as a tassel, a cocklebur, and a rope. Another woman is at the heart of "After Years," in which the poet uses first-person perspective to describe seeing someone who is far away and walking farther away. He is lonely because the person he would most like to tell about what he sees is the person moving away from him.

The next poem is also about someone's absence. In "Garage Sale," Kooser again uses the first-person perspective to describe shopping at a garage sale just as it begins to rain. The poet talks with the woman holding the sale and wonders where her husband is. He leaves with nothing, since none of the woman's husband's belongings are suited for him. The potential for loss permeates "Surviving," as the poet describes a ladybird beetle and sees how it reacts to the threat of death, as fearful as all living things.

After a brief visit by a sparrow in "A Glimpse of the Eternal," Kooser compares the fading importance of a love affair and the way memories change over time to the way land masses on the Earth move and re-form in "Tectonics." The collection ends with "A Happy Birthday." Written in first person, the poem describes the experience of reading a book in the evening until darkness overtakes the room. The poet does not turn on the light but continues to sit with the book in the dark.

Themes

The Human Condition

Many of the poems in *Delights & Shadows* explore various aspects of the human condition—what it means to be human in terms of common experiences and reactions to these experiences. In "Walking on Tiptoe," Kooser describes how the psychic weight of being human physically affects us: "There is little spring to our walk, *we are so burdened with responsibility."* This poem *differentiates humans from animals, a point also touched on in "In the Hall of Bones."* Here, the poet emphasizes how people are conscious of their humanity and suffer as a result. Kooser writes of humans, "*Of all the skeletons* assembled here, this is the only one *in which once throbbed a heart* made sad by brooding on its shadow."

Not all of Kooser's poems are as solemn. While the title of "At the Cancer Clinic" suggests illness, the poem itself is focused on the kindness of three people who assist and encourage a patient. Kooser writes that "Grace *fills the clean mold of this moment." In "Bank Fishing for Bluegills," Kooser compares an older fisherman in poor health to an aluminum boat and likens his physical decline to weightlessness: "His face has the flat gray sheen of a man* with a failing heart, but he is all lightness now, / and tethered only gently to this world."

A number of Kooser's poems about the human condition contain an air of sorrow, often related to broken or complicated connections between people. "The Beaded Purse" tells the sad story of a Midwestern father picking up his daughter's remains at a train station. She had left without his permission at the age of nineteen and claimed to have become a successful actress in the East, though the state of her body and possessions indicate otherwise. Despite the disconnect between the father and daughter, the father wants to protect his wife's memory of their daughter. He places some money in his daughter's purse for his wife to find and take comfort in. This gesture of protection distances the man from his wife and the truth. "Garage Sale" takes a more personal tone for Kooser, as he describes briefly chatting with a woman holding a garage sale as he helps her move some goods out of the rain. He notices some men's things, which are not suitable for him, or for anyone other than their original owner. He wonders where that man is, seeing the connection between husband and wife as conspicuous in its absence. He leaves with nothing: "I walk so empty-handed to my car."

Aging and Death

In this collection, the poet repeatedly explores the effects of time on the human body and mind. In "Tattoo," Kooser describes an older man's fading tattoo, and sees that while he still wants to seem tough, "he is only another old man, picking up / broken tools and putting them back, *his heart gone soft and blue with stories." "New Cap"* also describes the physical effects of aging on an old man, who has grown smaller over time, while "Home Medical Dictionary" emphasizes the book's use as *"an atlas for the old,* in which they pore over *the pink and gray maps of the body."* "A Spiral Notebook" describes seeing a five-subject notebook in a drugstore and realizing that he has aged: "It *seems* a part of growing old is no longer/ to have five subjects, ... but instead to stand in a drugstore *and hang on to one subject* a little too long."

Kooser looks at death primarily as a phenomenon affecting the living, such as in "The Beaded Purse." In the short poem "The Mourners," he describes the events after a funeral, when the attendees are reluctant to part. At least three of the poems about death focus on the poet's parents. While "Pearl" focuses on his visit to an aged cousin to inform her of his mother's death, "Mother" offers Kooser's own feelings about his mother's passing as he describes what has happened in nature in the month since she died. He misses her but is grateful to her, saying, "Were it not for the way you taught me to look *at the world, to see the life at play in everything,* I would have to be lonely forever." Kooser shares similar sentiments in "Father," written on his long-deceased father's birthday. The poet imagines what life would be like if his father was still alive and is glad that he did not have to become fearful and feeble with age. However, Kooser misses him and is reminded of him by the lilacs blooming all around. The poet accepts death as an inevitable—and not-unwelcome—part of life.

The Past

A number of poems in *Delights & Shadows* describe events of the past. Kooser often draws on his own memories for inspiration, making the poems more personal. Certain poems in the collection refer to specific times in the past. "Creamed Corn" describes how Jamaican workers acted and were treated by Iowa locals when they came to work at a Green Giant plant during the 1940s, while "A Jacquard Shawl" details the title object, made in 1778 from the wool of sheep who lost their lives to a dog attack.

Kooser's recollections of the past are sometimes general and sometimes very specific. "Memory," for example, is a furious tornado of images sweeping through a farm, recalling the people and things that once belonged there. "Ice Cave" presents a set of memories associated with a specific place. In the past tense, Kooser describes a cave where people once stored ice cut from the river and spent hot summer days in the coolness. "Applesauce" is one of several poems that seem specific to Kooser's personal memories. In this poem, he offers his fond recollections of the way an older woman in Iowa made applesauce, clearly something he watched many times.

Style

Prose Poems

Many of the poems in *Delights & Shadows* are prose poems. These are poems that are not metered or rhymed and do not use traditional poetic line breaks. Even though prose poems use everyday language, they often employ some poetic elements, such as vivid imagery, repetition, and fragmentation. Prose poems can be of any length and focus on any subject. In Kooser's collection, "Surviving," "Flow Blue China," and "Screech Owl" are a few examples of prose poems.

Free Verse

Some of the poems in *Delights & Shadows* are written in free verse. This type of poetry does not use a specific kind of rhyme or meter—there is not a set limit to the number of syllables in a line, and there are no rules concerning the placement of stresses in the line. Instead, free verse employs a structure determined by the poet, in which the poem's pattern and line breaks make the piece look and sound like traditional versed poetry. Poems like "*Lobocraspis griseifusa*," "Cosmetics Department," and "A Jar of Buttons" are examples of free verse in *Delights & Shadows*.

Topics for Further Study

- Research the work of Mary Cassatt or Winslow Homer. Compare your impressions to Kooser's descriptions in "A Box of Pastels" or "Four Civil War Paintings by Winslow Homer." In a paper, describe your observations and reactions as informed by the poem.

- Reread "The Beaded Purse." What do you think the story in the poem about? Keeping your interpretation in mind, write your own narrative poem from the point of view of another character in Kooser's poem, such as the daughter, the mother, the station agent, or the father.

- The painting on the cover of the 2004 Copper Canyon Press edition of *Delights & Shadows* is "August Night at Russell's Corners" by George Ault. Kooser says of it, "There's a kind of strangeness about that image ... you don't know what's beyond the darkness. The painting says that if you can awaken inside the familiar and discover it strange, you need never leave home." Pick a poem in the collection that most evokes this feeling in you. In a small group, have each person share why the poem he or she selected represents this idea.

- Research African American history in Iowa. Focus your research on the lives of African Americans in that state during the first half of the twentieth century. Using your findings, discuss the origin, evolution, and legacy of the tensions described in "Creamed Corn."

- Explore Ted Kooser's nonfiction advice book for poets, *The Poetry Home Repair Manual: Practical Advice For Beginning Poets* (2005). Is his advice reflected in *Delights & Shadows*? How are examples of his advice present or absent in the works of other well-known poets, like Robert Frost or Langston Hughes? Research Kooser's advice and different poets' poetry individually, then, as a group, discuss how much you believe his wisdom applies in different cases.

Narrative Poems

Narrative poems tell stories. Narrative poems can be written in verse, but, as in Kooser's book, they can also be more like short stories. The most obvious narrative poem in *Delights & Shadows* is "The Beaded Purse." In this poem, Kooser tells the story of a father who has to pick up his estranged daughter's corpse at a train station. Kooser describes how the father takes it upon himself to put money in his daughter's purse to spare his wife unnecessary pain, because his daughter does not appear to have become a successful actress like she has led her mother to believe. "Pearl," a first-person account of visiting his mother's cousin to tell her of his mother's death, is another narrative poem in the collection.

Figurative Images

Koozser employs figurative images throughout *Delights & Shadows*. Such imagery does not describe things literally but is representational and symbolic. Metaphors and similes cast the poet's observations in terms of the familiar. The young man in "Student," for example, is compared to a turtle, and the old man in "Bank Fishing for Bluegills" is compared to a boat. The use of figurative images can describe something's appearance and add an emotional element to a poem. Figurative images can also help the reader understand and relate to the theme of a poem. In the poem "Memory," the funnel cloud-pen is a figurative image used to represent the surprising power of memories. "A Jar of Buttons" also uses this technique to convey history and hard work. It begins with the stanza: "This is a core sample / from the floor of the Sea of Mending."

Literal Images

Kooser uses literal images in *Delights & Shadows* as well as figurative ones. Literal images represent exactly what they describe. Literal images make poems more accessible to readers and often help them better understand the figurative language being used. For example, in "Applesauce," Kooser begins with "I liked how the starry blue lid / of that saucepan lifted and puffed." Readers can picture the lid of the saucepan, and with that image gain entrance into Kooser's more figurative descriptions in the rest of the poem, which concern the woman who is making the applesauce. When he describes the sailboats on her apron as "the only boats under sail / for at least two thousand miles," he uses a literal image to launch a figurative one that references their physical location in the Midwest.

Mood

Mood is the primary emotion a poem evokes. The poems in *Delights & Shadows* vary in their mood from celebratory ("A Box of Pastels") to angry ("Old Cemetery") to morose ("Home Medical Dictionary"). In the poems in which Kooser writes about his deceased parents, the mood is by turns somber and sentimental, as in "Mother" and "Father." Sometimes the mood is surprising considering the poem's subject. For example, "At the Cancer Clinic" and "The Old People" are both uplifting, comforting poems about people nearing the ends of their lives.

Historical Context

Nebraska

Kooser finds much of the inspiration for his writing in the state of Nebraska, where he has made his home for most of his adult life. He has lived for many years on a farm near the village of Garland. In many of the poems in *Delights & Shadows*, Kooser reflects on places or situations he has experienced in Nebraska. The state is not mentioned by name in any of the poems, but the culture, society, and values of Nebraska and the Great Plains have influenced his perception of the world and his writing.

Known as the "Cornhusker State," Nebraska has had primarily an agricultural and ranch-based economy since it became a part of the United States with the Louisiana Purchase in 1803. In its early days as a state, Nebraska was populated by Americans who were lured by the promises of the Homestead Act. In the Homestead Act of 1862, the federal government promised to give 160 acres of land to anyone who could pay a small fee and remain on the land for a specified period of time. Even the state's official seal attests to the importance of agriculture, with a farmer's cabin, wheat sheaves, and growing corn among its primary images.

Nearly 95 percent of Nebraska's land is

dedicated to farming and ranching, and about one-fifth of the state's workforce is employed in the agriculture industry. Corn and soybeans are two of the state's primary crops. In the late 1990s, the number of farms in Nebraska decreased, but the farms that remained were larger and often relied on mechanization to optimize output. Though drought hindered farm output in the first years of the twenty-first century, Nebraska remained the fourth most profitable state in agriculture in 2001, with cash receipts from the marketing of farm products totaling $9.5 billion.

Nebraska has been attempting to diversify its economy to ensure long-term financial stability, in part by encouraging an already large manufacturing industry. The state's population, however, has not changed rapidly. In 2002, population only increased about 1 percent over the previous year. Nebraska's demographic makeup is also relatively unchanged. As of 2002, more than 90 percent of Nebraskans were white, and about half the population was over the age of thirty-five.

Iowa

Iowa, Nebraska's neighbor to the east, also plays a role in Kooser's poetry and perception of the world. Nebraska and Iowa have much in common: Both were original parts of the Louisiana Purchase and both have a basically static population. Agriculture and ranching are two of Iowa's primary industries, with corn, soybeans, oats, and hay being the major farm products. To make a living from farming in Iowa, as in Nebraska, has required long hours and constant struggle.

In the early twentieth century, the number of farmers in Iowa decreased as mechanization lead to the creation of larger farms. Though the state had been a leading egg producer and had a significant number of milk cows, these farm industries essentially disappeared by 1960. In that year, more Iowans lived in urban areas than rural areas for the first time. Because of the uncertainties of a changing agricultural market, Iowa worked to diversify its economy after World War II. However, many of the state's major non-farming businesses are still related to agriculture, such as food processing, meat packing, and farm equipment manufacturing.

Dust Bowl

Several poems, including "Grasshoppers," in *Delights & Shadows* allude to the Dust Bowl of the 1930s. In the mid-1930s, at the height of the Great Depression in the United States, farmers in the Great Plains states faced economic disaster caused by an extended and harsh drought. From 1934 to 1938, the weather remained bone dry, extremely windy, and intensely hot during the seasons when crops usually grow the most. During this time period, intense wind storms removed the dry topsoil from farmland in states affected by the drought, further eroding the economy and spreading dust over large parts of the country. While Nebraska and Iowa were not at the center of the Dust Bowl—Kansas and Oklahoma bore the brunt of the disaster—the drought and dust storms caused economic and social hardships for Nebraskans and Iowans as well.

Critical Overview

Critics have generally regarded Kooser's *Delights & Shadows* as representative of his poetry as whole: sparely written and accessible, with powerful imagery that explores the unexpected in the small events of everyday life. Reviewing the book for the website ninetyandnine.com, David Bunch wrote,

> He continually grabs the reader's attention by taking a seemingly ordinary event or observation, placing it into what at first glance could be an ordinary poem, and then turning it all on its head by linking it with something so striking that the reader is faced head-on with the enormity of reality.

One aspect of Kooser's work that has gained much critical attention is the craft and depth of the collection as a whole. Calling the poems "understated, more plain than pretty," Elizabeth Lund of the *Christian Science Monitor* also noted that "what's most remarkable about this book ... is the consistency of tone and quality. Page after page illumines small moments." Similarly, Kathleen de Grave of the *Midwest Quarterly* commented, "*Delights & Shadows* is a book that can be read more than once, for the immediacy of color and line, and then again, for the generosity of its vision."

A few critics found fault with the poetry in

Delights & Shadows and with the poet's own outlook on life. Brian Phillips of *Poetry* quibbled with the notion that the literature of the Great Plains necessarily demands plain language. The critic believed that "there is some quaintness in Kooser's new book," which he argued "comes more from Kooser's outlook than from any particular flaw in his use of rural Nebraska settings or his plainspoken register."

While Jeffrey Galbraith of the *Harvard Review* found much to like in the collection, the reviewer noted, "sentiment is one of the weak spots in the otherwise splendid *Delights & Shadows*." Gailbraith elaborates, "With a few notable exceptions, *Delights & Shadows* is most rewarding when Kooser is not directly involved in the poem but watching from a distance. In this position, the poet finds magic in activities and objects typically considered mundane."

What Do I Read Next?

- *Winter Morning Walks: One Hundred Postcards to Jim Harrison* (2000) is another collection of poetry written by Kooser. The book of poems, inspired by Kooser's morning walks as he recovered from cancer, won the 2001 Nebraska Book Award for Poetry.

- *Local Wonders: Seasons in the Bohemian Alps* (2002) is a collection of essays by Kooser. This book was the Winner of the Nebraska Book Award for Nonfiction in 2003 and consists of essays about the author's life and the area in which he lives.

- *Weather Central*, published by the University of Pittsburgh Press in 1994, is a collection of Kooser's poems. The poet has identified this collection as his personal favorite.

- In an effort to increase the popularity of poetry in the United States, Kooser created a website, www.americanlifeinpoetry.org, which regularly features new American poets. This website is related to his column "American Life in Poetry," which is available for free to any publication.

- *Braided Creek: A Conversation in Poetry* (2003) is a collection Kooser wrote with Jim Harrison. Winner of the 2003 Award for Poetry from the Society of Midland Authors, the book contains poems that the two writers exchanged with one another during Kooser's recovery from cancer.

- *The Art of Drowning* (1995) is a volume of poetry by Billy Collins, U.S. Poet Laureate from 2001 to 2003. Like Kooser, Collins uses straightforward, approachable language to explore nature and life's little details. Collins is known for his wit and warmth and is one of the country's best-known and best-loved poets.

- Poet William Carlos Williams (1883–1963) pioneered the use of clear imagery and plain language in poetry in the United States. *William Carlos Williams: Selected Poems* (2004) introduces the reader to Williams's uniquely American voice and his poetry of everyday events.

Sources

Bunch, David, Review of *Delights & Shadows*, Ninetyandnine.com, www.ninetyandnine.com/Archives/20050613/review (April 1, 2006).

De Grave, Kathleen, Review of *Delights & Shadows*, in the *Midwest Quarterly*, Vol. 46, No. 4, Summer 2005, p. 439.

Galbraith, Jeffrey, "Local Wonders," in the *Harvard Review*, Vol. 28, June 2005, p. 183.

Kooser, Ted, *Delights & Shadows*, Copper Canyon Press, 2004.

Lund, Elizabeth, "The Power of a Gentle Rain," in the *Christian Science Monitor*, April 26, 2005, p. 16.

McKee, Louis, Review of *Delights & Shadows*, in *Library Journal*, Vol. 129, No. 3, February 15, 2004, p. 130.

Phillips, Brian, Review of *Delights & Shadows*, in *Poetry*, Vol. 185, No. 5, February 2005, p. 396.

Roberts-Gudeman, Kim, "A Poet's Inspiration," in the *Omaha World-Herald* (Omaha, NB), April 9, 2005, p. 1E.

"Straight Answers from Ted Kooser," in *American Libraries*, Vol. 35, No. 11, December 2004, p. 31.

Further Reading

Cikovsky, Nicolai, et. al., *Winslow Homer*, Yale University Press, 1995.

> This biography explores the life of Winslow Homer, whose paintings are the subject of a four-part poem in *Delights & Shadows*.

Frazier, Ian, *Great Plains*, Picador, 2001.

> Frazier chronicles his explorations of the whole of the Great Plains, offering his experiences as a traveler as well as information about local culture and history.

Kooser, Ted, *The Poetry Home Repair Manual: Practical Advice for Beginning Poets*, University of Nebraska Press, 2005.

> In this collection of Kooser's essays, he offers advice for those who want to express themselves through poetry.

Kooser, Ted, and Steve Cox, *Writing Brave and Free: Encouraging Words for People Who Want to Start Writing*, Bison, 2006.

> The second of Kooser's how-to books, this volume offers gentle encouragement and practical advice to would-be writers.

Maharidge, Dale, and Michael Williamson, *Denison, Iowa: Searching for the Soul of America Through the Secrets of a Midwest Town*, Free Press, 2005.

> In this nonfiction book, the authors examine how changes over the course of a year in the town of Denison have affected the community, focusing primarily on economic decline and shifting demographics.

Whye, Mike, *Nebraska Simply Beautiful*, Farcountry Press, 2004.

> This book contains photographs of Nebraska's diverse landscape.

Printed in the USA
CPSIA information can be obtained
at www.ICGtesting.com
LVHW011944180823
755411LV00013B/750